Made in the USA
Columbia, SC
09 January 2022

53965283R00067